Understanding the Role of Suffering and:

Rising Above The Pain

Strength to handle life's problems, increase God-Esteem, and walk in victory!

By:

Michelle Olivia Smith

<u>Dedication</u>

To my husband, Samuel Titus Smith, with all my love.
Thank you for your unfailing support.

__Acknowledgements__

To my Lord and Savior Jesus Christ, thank you for teaching me what I needed to know to conquer my trials and tribulations and to rise above the pain. Thank you for molding me and making me, and inspiring me to write this book. I am nothing without you. It is because of you that I walk in victory.

To my loving husband, I cannot thank you enough for encouraging me, helping me, and for not letting me lose sight of my goal. As we stated to each other at our wedding, you are my Tree and I am your Leaves, with our roots in Christ, we flourish as one in Him.

To my "editorial staff": Sis. Shirley Stewart, Sis. Nicole Kenan, my mother, Elizabeth J. Young, and my husband, Jr. Deacon Samuel Titus Smith, you are the best! Thank you for helping make this book better. Your feedback and suggestions were greatly appreciated. To Mother Sandra M. Jones of Brooklyn New York, thank you for your timely encouragement that truly blessed my soul.

To my former pastor, Bishop Lymus Johnson, and all the saints at Refuge Church of Christ in Philadelphia PA: You rallied around me, prayed for me, and helped me through some of the most intense pain of my life. "Thank you" is not enough, but God will reward you for your labor of love.

To my current pastor and assistant pastor, Bishop William L. Bonner and Elder W. Michael Fields, thank you for your excellent preaching and teaching. Because of you I have left drinking milk, and have matured to eating the meat of the Word. To all the saints at Refuge Temple Church of Our Lord Jesus Christ in Washington DC, thank you for your prayers, encouragement and support.

To my parents, Elizabeth and Oliver G.C. Young, who always believed in me, always encouraged me, never suppressed my creativity, but always celebrated my accomplishments: thank you, thank you, thank you! You two were my very first blessing, and I am eternally grateful to God for wonderful parents like you. This book was possible, in large part, because you were the first to teach me about faith in God. I love you.

4

Contents

INTRODUCTION

THE STORM

It starts…
Like any other.
Thunder rolls from afar.
And the wind, which once was a gentle breeze,
Comes in gusts as it blows through the trees
And lightning lives up to its name as it lights up the sky
And the storm,
Like any other,
Passes by.

- Michelle Smith
(written in the 3rd grade)

When you are newly saved, you are a lot like a blank piece of white paper. So clean and pure, cleaner than you ever thought possible. The Holy Ghost has come in and sanctified you. You are on a honeymoon with the Lord, and walking on air. Light as a feather, you float, just like a piece of paper floats on air as it wafts down to the ground….

Then storms and trials come, as they must if we are to know Christ in the fellowship of His suffering, These tests that give us testimonies sometimes double us over, like bending a piece of paper. Some tests turn us every which way, and we are taken out of our comfort zone, bending over backwards. Some fiery trials that come cut you on every side. Sometimes these situations leave you bent, but not broken, and cut, but not killed. You might ask, what is the purpose of it all?

Then the Lord speaks to your mind, "Trouble won't last always; they that sew in tears shall reap in joy[1]" And when the storm passes over, and the sun shines again, you unfold, rise, and stretch. But you are no longer the flat blank piece of paper. You float a little lighter, you weigh a little less, little pieces are gone in all the right places, and you are a beautiful

---

[1] See Psalms 126:5

snowflake, unique and special (no two snowflakes are exactly alike). All that you have gone through has made you into what you are today…

It is my hope that the pages of this book will help you, no matter what state you are in. If you are in the midst of the storm, or just coming out of it, or if you have been wandering in a wilderness for quite some time, I hope you will find peace and understanding through this book. If skies are sunny, I hope you will gain the tools to prepare for your coming storms, for if you name the name of Christ, storms will surely come. The Word of God tells us however, that they that sew in tears shall reap in joy, and our God takes us from victory to victory. Hopefully this book will help you get to your next victory a little faster, as you understand the role of suffering and learn to Rise Above The Pain.

A PERSONAL TESTIMONY

It was Sunday, November 14, 1993. My parents, my fiancé, his parents and siblings arrived at the church. There was joy, anticipation, and happiness in the air. Over 6 and ½ years of friendship, fellowship, and love were going to be celebrated on this day. I handed the ushers little cards to pass out to the congregation. The cards said:

You are cordially invited to witness a joyous event
in the lives of our children
Michelle Olivia Young
and
Perry Miller
immediately following morning service

Mr. & Mrs. Oliver Young
and
Mrs. Dorothy Miller

The Date To Remember:
June 11, 1994

I was getting married! I had been saved since the young age of 15, and had finished high school and college. At 24 years old, I was looking forward to sharing my life with the man I loved. I met Perry in my senior year of high school. He was kind, handsome, and strong, and in time he began attending my church. He was a marine reservist, a wonderful cook, an artist, a clothing designer, and a sensitive man with a hearty laugh and a handsome smile. He worked faithfully with the young people, the prison ministry, and labored on local and national levels in our church organization. We sang in the same choir, and, in the fullness of time, we fell in love. Six years and eight months after we first met, we went up in front of the church to announce our engagement.

We had come to the church on that November morning, all dressed up, and full of joy. Little did I know that my fiancé would have a surprise for me that day. As we stood in front of the church, he had 6 ushers walk down the aisle toward me. Each usher carried a half dozen peach and red roses. As they walked past me, each usher handed me a rose bouquet. Mother Eloise Mosley, one of the dear mothers of our church, read a statement that my fiancé had written to me. An excerpt from that statement is as follows:

"……..for many years I have searched, for true love is hard to find in a world like this. But God has shown me that true love exists, and you are His example. From that point on I have loved you and will always love you. If God will fulfill one desire of my heart as I seek Him in all His righteousness, it is that when we get to heaven, He would allow me to remember you, so that I can love again for all eternity."

We were like them that dream. I was walking on air. I was absolutely the happiest young woman on the face of the earth. We took many pictures that day. The entire church shared in our joy. Many looking back on the pictures of the wedding announcement said it was as though we were wed that day….they just couldn't wait to see what the actual wedding would be like!

*   *   *

The morning of Monday, December 20, 1993 started much like any other day. I got up, and went to work. They were having a Christmas party on the job, but for some reason I didn't feel much like socializing. I got some food, and went back to my desk to sit down to work. There I sat, all by myself. I didn't feel my usual bubbly self, but I shrugged it off, and continued going about my day. That evening when I got home, I received a phone call. My wedding invitations were ready! I just needed to come pick them up! I was in the middle of the phone call when my parents asked me to put down the phone

9

because they needed to talk to me. I came into my parents' room, and sat down on their bed. My mother sat on my left, and my father sat on my right. My mother then told me something terrible happened to Perry. They said that he had had a massive heart attack that morning.

The news got me to my feet. "Ok, lets go to the hospital!" I said. But nobody moved. I said, "Come on let's go......He is alright, isn't he?.....Tell me he is alright!" My mother then told me Perry had gone to be with the Lord...

*   *   *

Nothing I had been through up until that time, and nothing that I have gone through since, can compare to the suffering I experienced through that trial. My whole world turned upside down. All of my plans, hopes and dreams were shattered. The direction my life was moving in had been halted. Suddenly. Unexpectedly. I was in shock. I was numb. Surely this was a dream, surely this was a horrible nightmare. Any moment now I would wake up and call my soon to be husband and tell him all about this. I expected him to walk in at any time so I could tell him this preposterous story that people had been telling me about him dying of a heart attack.....As the days passed, however, it became clear that the "dream" was reality.

The saints of God gathered around me, and did all they could to comfort me. My church family was there for me in such a significant way, I do not believe I could ever properly thank them. Our Lord will reward them when we see Him in peace. They visited me, they prayed for me, they encouraged me. They cried with me, they sat with me, they cared for me. Their outpouring of love will never be forgotten. In the midst of it all, I tried to cope. But I had questions. Why did this happen to me? Had I done anything wrong? Why would God allow this to occur? What did the future hold for me? What was God's will for my life?

I needed answers, and I was desperate for them. So I did something I had never done. I went on a *long* fast. No solid food, no food at all, for ten days. I drank water, I even chewed gum to keep my breath sweet. My mother, worried about me, insisted that I eat something on the tenth day, so I actually made it through about 9 and ¾ of a day.....but still the Lord began to open up my understanding. In the weeks that followed, the Lord began to help me understand that all things were still working together for my good. He showed me how to rise above the pain. The following February, in 1994, I became a junior missionary, and I now serve as a senior missionary in my local church. My grieving process and recovery was gradual, over time, but I had a Wonderful Counselor, a Mighty God, an Everlasting Father, A Prince Of Peace. It was not easy, but it was not meant to be. The trial that I endured was meant for a purpose: To strengthen me in Christ so that I could become strong enough to help somebody else.

For many years I felt if I could reverse the situation, I would. But I finally came to the point where I knew that I would not trade what I had learned about my Lord in my walk with Him to bring my espoused husband back. Through this trial, the Lord taught me what it means to totally trust in Him for my waking up every day, for my breathing in and out, for my going out and my coming in, for my life, health and strength. He showed me that He **could** wipe the tears from my eyes, and that He **could** bear my burdens. As long as I lean on Him, He will be my source of strength and my refuge in times of trouble. My trust, my hope, and my confidence are in Him, and in Him I live, move, and have my being. I am complete in Him who is the head of all principality and power. And as I work for the up building of His Kingdom, seeking that first, and seeking His righteousness, I know that all my needs and all my desires (Which He gives to me in the first place) will be supplied. Like

Job, I can now truly say, years later: The Lord giveth, and the Lord taketh away, blessed be the Name of the Lord!

I knew then, as I know now, that the key to my spiritual survival was learning to say "Hallelujah anyhow". Learning to praise God in the midst of my pain. Learning to thank God, thank him for everything - even my trials. This was the only way out of my suffering. It takes faith and trust to continue to serve and praise God in spite of your situation. Praise begets joy, and the joy of the Lord is your strength! The Holy Ghost is truly a Pain Reliever and a Comforter. Through my test, I got to know Christ in a way that I had not previously known Him. He suffered, bled and died for us. If we are to be like Him, we must also know suffering. If you trust Him, God will get you through your trial, He will teach you how to cope, and He will make you strong. Through the fellowship of His suffering, I learned many things about rising above the pain:

1. ***Don't charge God foolishly.*** God is for you. He is your friend. He knows the end from the beginning, and all things really do work together for the good of them who love the Lord. All His thoughts toward us are positive, and no good thing will he withhold from them who walk upright. Always remember this. Refuse to believe anything else. Don't allow anger at God to cause you to sin. Yes, He allowed it to happen, but it is for a greater purpose, and His love for you has never wavered. He knew it would happen before it did, and He is already working to help you to cope, and to help you grow from your experience. He loves you, and because He loves you He must fulfill His will in your life. He has many blessings to give you, but you cannot receive them until you are ready. Your trials are one of the things God uses to get you ready.

2. ***God is not trying to kill you.*** He is trying to give you the tools to live eternally. He is teaching you how to fight the good fight of faith, leaning on the Lord, and not to your own understanding. Many times He takes us

12

through suffering because He has so much in store for us, but first He has to mold us into the person that can make the most out of our blessings. We need to have the full understanding of His plan for our lives, and that understanding sometimes must come through tests and trials. The Word tells us that joy comes in the morning, and I can personally testify to you that this is true. If we would just hold out until our tomorrow comes, we would be astonished at what God will do in our lives.

3. ***It is OK to ask for understanding.*** Some say: "Don't question God". I say: " Don't put your hands on you're hips and move your neck (or wag your finger) at God". Proverbs chapter 4, verse 5 says, "Get wisdom, get understanding..." The Lord wants to help you cope, He wants you to understand the "why" of things. Be patient, and ask Him to open up your understanding and speak to your heart. He will do it, if you humbly ask. The only thing better than the wisdom and understanding you will gain from enduring adversity, is the closer relationship with the Lord that you will develop though trials and tribulations.

4. ***Feed on The Word.*** This may seem elementary, but it is crucial. All you need is in the Word of God, and in reading and studying God's Word, we put ourselves in a position to be ministered to by God. The Scripture is powerful, and will help you rise above the pain, no matter what the source of that pain is. The Word will help you keep your eyes and mind on Christ. The Bible is our weapon, our sword. It will help us fight negative or erroneous thinking when we are tested and tried.

5. ***Continue to be faithful.*** If people have caused the suffering, don't take revenge – it is not yours to take. Render good for evil – no matter how hard it is. If problems or sickness caused the suffering, continue to trust in and serve God as much, or more than before

the problem arrived! If you are in a wilderness experience, wait on the Lord, be of good courage. Ask Him to teach you what you need to learn through this so you can come out of the wilderness. Show the Lord, yourself, others, and the devil, that you will not be defeated. Be not weary in well doing, as the Word says, and you will quickly rise above the pain of your situation. What do I mean by "a wilderness experience"? We will address that later in the book . But right now, lets try to understand the important role suffering plays in our lives…

*   *   *

THE ROLE OF SUFFERING

Philippians 3: 8-11
[8]Yea doubtless, and I count all things but loss for the excellency of the knowledge of Christ Jesus my Lord: for whom I have suffered the loss of all things, and do count them but dung, that I may win Christ,

[9]And be found in him, not having mine own righteousness, which is of the law, but that which is through the faith of Christ, the righteousness which is of God by faith:

[10]That I may know him, and the power of his resurrection, and the fellowship of his sufferings, being made conformable unto his death;

[11]If by any means I might attain unto the resurrection of the dead.

What does suffering accomplish? It makes us strong. It helps us to become more like Christ. It helps us to know the Lord better. As saved people, it is essential that we have a close relationship with the Father. We want to do His will, and His work, we have to get to know Him in order to find out what that will is. Part of knowing Christ, part of becoming like Jesus, part of becoming intimately acquainted, is to suffer with Him. In doing so, we share in His sufferings. We become like Him. Like He was when He suffered, even until His death on the cross, not being concerned about the shame of what he endured. He was not offended by the fulfillment of His destiny. We must not be offended by our suffering.

2 Timothy 2:10-12a
[10]Therefore I endure all things for the elect's sakes, that they may also obtain the salvation which is in Christ Jesus with eternal glory.

[11]It is a faithful saying: For if we be dead with him, we shall also live with him:
[12]If we suffer, we shall also reign with him

If you have ever been in a love relationship with the opposite sex, you know that going through hardship together brings you closer. Going through hardship with the Lord will also bring you closer. You cannot truly appreciate how good God has been in your life until He has delivered you out of something, or helped you to endure through it. We, the church[2], are the Savior's bride. As we remain faithful "come what may" our relationship with the Bridegroom becomes stronger.

2 Timothy 2:3
[3]Thou therefore endure hardness, as a good soldier of Jesus Christ.

*   *   *

The days following my fiancé's death were unlike anything I had experienced. I seemed to be moving about, doing normal things. Getting up, getting dressed, coming downstairs, eating breakfast…but it felt like I was just watching myself do these things. I felt detached. Food was tasteless. I felt detached from reality. I could only escape in my dreams. You see, when I slept I would dream of my beloved, but then I would wake up, and realize it was a dream, and he was gone again.

One day, my mother and I went to Perry's mother's house to talk about the funeral arrangements. On the way over in the car the Holy Spirit told me to say 'Hallelujah'. I thought, "I can't say that! I don't want to say that! How can you ask me to say that under these circumstances?" However, in my spirit I

---

[2] Are you in the church? Are you in the Savior's Bride? See the Appendix to be certain!

16

knew I had to. I had to praise God in spite of the situation. I knew the Lord still loved me. His hand was still on my life. I could not let my circumstance interfere with praising my God. So I did. I whispered "hallelujah". I said it again. I felt a little better. The more I praised Him, the more I knew that my healing was in the praise. I kept praising God, and the Holy Ghost kept comforting me. In the weeks and months that followed, it was the praise and worship of God and the sweet anointing of the Holy Ghost, that helped me rise above the pain.

Here is a poem I wrote that talks about why we have suffering in our lives. A good friend of mine once told me: "Time and chance come to everyone." That means that every person has a season of suffering. It is though this time that we are proven, and we are refined in the fire.

God Wants To Prove You

Wondering why you are going through?
It is necessary! God wants to prove you!
Prove that Him only you will serve
That you will stand, and take Him at His Word.
Always remember His promise to you,
Remaining faithful, remaining true.
Resolve right now that you will stand
Holding on until you reach the promised land!
Believe in your heart, it won't be long,
God will give you a brand new song!
Rejoice in the day that He has made,
Letting Him guide you along the way.

It is easy to serve God when everything is wonderful. However, can He trust you to serve Him when times get tough? Nobody needs a 'fair-weather friend'. Why do you serve Him? For what He can do for you? Or for who He is, and what He has already done? If He never brings you out of your situation, would you continue to love Him?

*   *   *

GOD-ESTEEM:

YOUR ATTITUDE ABOUT GOD

God-esteem is a concept the Lord gave me one day. I began to notice the things that people say about God, the confessions that people make with their mouths, and began to realize that our thinking about God affects our relationship with him. It is hard to have a good relationship with someone who does not think much of you. God-esteem also directly affects our ability to rise above the pain of trials and tribulations. The enemy of our souls wants us to think that God doesn't love us because He allowed pain and suffering to touch our lives. If we buy into the lies of the devil, we will think some destructive things about God, and will have low God-esteem.

If you think God hates you, or is against you, how can you fathom His awesome love and grace?

If you think God is not thinking about you, or He is punishing you, how can you respond positively to him?

Let's further define what we mean by this concept of God-Esteem. Let's start by looking at the word *esteem:*

Main Entry: [2]**esteem**
Function: transitive verb
Etymology: Middle English estemen to estimate, from Middle French estimer, from Latin aestimare
1 archaic : **APPRAISE**
2 a : to view as : **CONSIDER** <esteem it a privilege> **b :** **THINK, BELIEVE**
3 : to set a high value on : regard highly and prize accordingly
synonym see REGARD[3]

---

[3] Source: http://www.m-w.com/cgi-bin/dictionary

Notice that synonyms of this word are THINK and BELIEVE. We know without faith it is impossible to please God, and so this is key to our relationship with Him. If you don't think very much of someone, it comes across in your actions and your words. If you don't respect them or regard them highly, it is noticeable.

You may think to yourself, "Of course I esteem God!" it may be difficult to ask yourself the question or to truly consider if your God-esteem is where it should be. Remember, however, we are human, and we don't always understand what God is doing. The Bible says we see through a glass darkly.....we know in part and we prophesy in part[4]. As long as we are in the flesh, we will not have 100% wisdom, knowledge, or understanding of all things. This is why we cannot please God without faith. You cannot have faith in someone you do not esteem.

Consider this carefully: how you think about God is going to determine your quality of life. He wants only the best for us, and He stands ready to meet every need. God is on our side! He loves us tremendously! Our attitude toward Him must reflect his love. You know the old song: 'Oh how I love Jesus, because He first loved me!'[5] How is your God-esteem? Are you hurting? Has the enemy tried to make you think God is against you? He is the father of liars. God loved you first! Be honest with yourself. Think about your level of God-esteem and what you think about God and His role in your life. If there are negative attitudes the enemy has put in your mind, confess them, and reject them!

There are times when God will test your esteem of Him. He is not always going to reveal the whole story to you, but He wants you to trust Him and hold out to see what the end is going to be. We have an example of this in the Word of God:

---

[4] See I Corinthians 13:9
[5] By Frederick Whitefield (1829-1904)

[47] *Verily, verily, I say unto you, He that believeth on me hath everlasting life.*

[48] *I am that bread of life.*

[49] *Your fathers did eat manna in the wilderness, and are dead.*

[50] *This is the bread which cometh down from heaven, that a man may eat thereof, and not die.*

[51] *I am the living bread which came down from heaven: if any man eat of this bread, he shall live for ever: and the bread that I will give is my flesh, which I will give for the life of the world.*

[52] *The Jews therefore strove among themselves, saying, How can this man give us his flesh to eat?*

[53] *Then Jesus said unto them, Verily, verily, I say unto you, Except ye eat the flesh of the Son of man, and drink his blood, ye have no life in you.*

[54] *Whoso eateth my flesh, and drinketh my blood, hath eternal life; and I will raise him up at the last day.*

[55] *For my flesh is meat indeed, and my blood is drink indeed.*

[56] *He that eateth my flesh, and drinketh my blood, dwelleth in me, and I in him.*

[57] *As the living Father hath sent me, and I live by the Father: so he that eateth me, even he shall live by me.*

[58] *This is that bread which came down from heaven: not as your fathers did eat manna, and are dead: he that eateth of this bread shall live for ever.*

[59] *These things said he in the synagogue, as he taught in Capernaum.*

[60] *Many therefore of his disciples, when they had heard this, said, This is an hard saying; who can hear it?*

[61] *When Jesus knew in himself that his disciples murmured at it, he said unto them, Doth this offend you?*

[62] *What and if ye shall see the Son of man ascend up where he was before?*

[63] *It is the spirit that quickeneth; the flesh profiteth nothing:*

the words that I speak unto you, they are spirit, and they are life.

⁶⁴ But there are some of you that believe not. For Jesus knew from the beginning who they were that believed not, and who should betray him.

⁶⁵ And he said, Therefore said I unto you, that no man can come unto me, except it were given unto him of my Father.

⁶⁶ From that time many of his disciples went back, and walked no more with him.

⁶⁷ Then said Jesus unto the twelve, Will ye also go away?

⁶⁸ Then Simon Peter answered him, Lord, to whom shall we go? thou hast the words of eternal life.

⁶⁹ And we believe and are sure that thou art that Christ, the Son of the living God.

Simon Peter had good God-esteem. He said it in the 68th and 69th verses. We need to be like Peter! No matter what the circumstances, no matter what the situation, no matter what the storm in our lives, we must know that HE WONT FAIL!! There is nowhere to go, there is no one else that can help us but GOD!!!

I have been in the midst of circumstances that seemed to me to be impossible. Whether it was people, sickness or problems; and sometimes it was lack. The lack of something I desired, something I was striving for and could not attain. The Lord only gave it to me when I let it go, and just began to trust. We can't get anything by ourselves. We can't maneuver anything, or force anything to come. If we do, it always messes up in the end. We cannot enjoy what we have obtained in an unrighteous way. There are times when you have to lay on your face and cry out to the Lord in faith. There are times when I have said, "Lord if you don't bless me I just won't be blessed, and if you don't help me I just won't be helped." In saying this I was telling the Lord the same thing as Simon Peter, but in a different way. I know that there is no other source of help, there is no one else that has the power to fix what is wrong. I am His child, and I won't disown Him. Whether He does it or not, I still know He is able. I know He can make a way. I am subject to His will, and I willingly have given Him my life. I know He will bless me, I know He will make it alright, and , no matter what the outcome, I know His perfect will is what is best for me! The Bible tells me in Zephaniah 3:17:

[17] The LORD thy God in the midst of thee is mighty; he will save, he will rejoice over thee with joy; he will rest in his love, he will joy over thee with singing.

He will save! He is my doctor, He is my lawyer, and He is my friend that sticks closer than a brother. He is the one that knows my heart and my mind. In the midst of my imperfection, He stretched his hands and died that I might be set free. He is planning my future, He is thinking about me, He is my provider, my healer and my helper. He is my encourager, my strength to go through. He is my battleaxe in the time of trouble. He is my refuge and my fortress. He is my God and in Him will I trust!

Through my trials I have learned that God won't fail. Even when I don't understand, He still has not failed. He knows what is best for me. In 1993 when my fiancé died less than six months prior to our wedding, little did I know that the Lord had a beautiful, marvelous marriage in store for me ten years later. I was disappointed when a job I was trying to get did not come through in 1991, but little did I know that He had a career for me that would allow me to eventually work with the surgeon general of the Coast Guard, and influence the culture and work processes of an important company. I fell on major financial difficulties when I got out of college, but little did I know He would make a way for me to be a homeowner 11 years later. Every test can become a testimony. It is not the suffering itself, but our response to the suffering that builds character, and helps us rise above the pain. The next time you are tested and tried, remember that this is part of God's divine plan. Resolve that you will respond with faith, prayer, praise, and a determination to go through it with God.

When I think of all the things that God has brought me through, I feel like David when he wrote in Psalms 98:1:

¹ O sing unto the LORD a new song; for he hath done marvellous things: his right hand, and his holy arm, hath gotten him the victory.

Think about your own tests that have become testimonies. What have they shown you? I hope by remembering what God has done for you and by hearing some of the things God has done for me, that you are encouraged to walk all the way with the Lord. The Bible says in I Corinthians 15:56-58:

⁵⁶ The sting of death is sin; and the strength of sin is the law. ⁵⁷ But thanks be to God, which giveth us the victory through our Lord Jesus Christ. ⁵⁸ Therefore, my beloved brethren, be ye stedfast, unmoveable, always abounding in the work of the Lord, forasmuch as ye know that your labour is not in vain in the Lord.

And also in Psalms 56:4:

⁴ In God I will praise his word, in God I have put my trust; I will not fear what flesh can do unto me.

And in Psalm 62:8:

⁸ Trust in him at all times; ye people, pour out your heart before him: God is a refuge for us. Selah.

Trust in God, be steadfast, unmovable. Your labor is not in vain! Your powerful, capable God is able to work your situation out! As holy people trusting in God, your assignment is to keep nourishing your God-esteem. You will overcome the enemy by the blood of the Lamb and by the word of your testimony. Your testimony is important. It consists of what you say to others about God. What you speak starts with what you think. Your thoughts influence your speech. Keep in mind how the Lord has fought your battles in the past, and is blessing you this very moment! Believe in His love for you, and His concern for your personal situation. Believe God, no matter how long it takes. His time is not our time, and His ways are not our ways, but you can believe that He will bring things out all right. Give that family member over to Him in prayer, trust him in your sickness and your suffering. He won't fail. Co-workers fail, friends fail, family fails, husbands fail, pastors fail, but **HE WON'T FAIL!!!**

Remember the story of Jehoshaphat, king of Judah? Jehoshaphat was an ally of Israel, and the Bible tells us in II Chronicles 22:9 that he sought the Lord with all his heart. He sought to stamp out idolatry, or the worship of any god other than the one true God of Israel. The 20th Chapter of II Chronicles shows us what Jehoshaphat did when confronted with an imminent attack by a group of nations consisting of the Moabites, Ammonites, and the children of Mount Seir.

II Chronicles 20
¹ It came to pass after this also, that the children of Moab, and the children of Ammon, and with them other beside the Ammonites, came against Jehoshaphat to battle.
² Then there came some that told Jehoshaphat, saying, There cometh a great multitude against thee from beyond the sea on this side Syria; and, behold, they be in Hazazontamar, which is Engedi.
³ And Jehoshaphat feared, and set himself to seek the LORD, and proclaimed a fast throughout all Judah.
⁴ And Judah gathered themselves together, to ask help of the LORD: even out of all the cities of Judah they came to seek the LORD.

What do you do when trouble surrounds you? The fear response, although not coming from God, is an understandable emotion. But we must get past that natural tendency to fear, and, like Jehoshaphat, seek the LORD! He remembered who God is, and he expressed his God-esteem in the scriptures:

5 And Jehoshaphat stood in the congregation of Judah and Jerusalem, in the house of the LORD, before the new court,
6 And said, O LORD God of our fathers, art not thou God in heaven? and rulest not thou over all the kingdoms of the heathen? and in thine hand is there not power and might, so that none is able to withstand thee?
7 Art not thou our God, who didst drive out the inhabitants of this land before thy people Israel, and gavest it to the seed of Abraham thy friend for ever?
8 And they dwelt therein, and have built thee a sanctuary therein for thy name, saying,
9 If, when evil cometh upon us, as the sword, judgment, or pestilence, or famine, we stand before this house, and in thy presence, (for thy name is in this house,) and cry unto thee in our affliction, then thou wilt hear and help.

We have to give the Word back to God! In faith, we must pray and let God know that we remember His promises to us, and we count Him to be worthy who promised. Jehoshaphat knew that if he cried unto the Lord, God would help him! We must take our burdens to the Lord in prayer! Tell Him our problems. Knowing that He will solve them! This is a true example of high God-esteem. That is what Jehoshaphat did:

10 And now, behold, the children of Ammon and Moab and mount Seir, whom thou wouldest not let Israel invade, when they came out of the land of Egypt, but they turned from them, and destroyed them not;
11 Behold, I say, how they reward us, to come to cast us out of thy possession, which thou hast given us to inherit.
12 O our God, wilt thou not judge them? for we have no

25

might against this great company that cometh against us; neither know we what to do: but our eyes are upon thee.
13   And all Judah stood before the LORD, with their little ones, their wives, and their children.

When you don't know what to do, call on God. Look to God, esteem Him able to help you, know that He won't fail you. He will give you the answer and tell you what to do. He will strengthen and encourage you, like He did Jahaziel:

14   Then upon Jahaziel the son of Zechariah, the son of Benaiah, the son of Jeiel, the son of Mattaniah, a Levite of the sons of Asaph, came the Spirit of the LORD in the midst of the congregation;
15   And he said, Hearken ye, all Judah, and ye inhabitants of Jerusalem, and thou king Jehoshaphat, Thus saith the LORD unto you, Be not afraid nor dismayed by reason of this great multitude; for the battle is not yours, but God's.
16   To morrow go ye down against them: behold, they come up by the cliff of Ziz; and ye shall find them at the end of the brook, before the wilderness of Jeruel.
17   Ye shall not need to fight in this battle: set yourselves, stand ye still, and see the salvation of the LORD with you, O Judah and Jerusalem: fear not, nor be dismayed; to morrow go out against them: for the LORD will be with you.

He told them that he would be with them. How much more will God be with you? He has given you the Holy Ghost, and has saved you. (Unsaved? See Appendix A in this book.) He did not come into your life just to let you down. He will be with you. He will bless you. He will provide for you. **He won't fail.**

And when the Holy Ghost has given us this kind of assurance, what else is there to do but worship Him, and praise His name? Just like Judah did:

18   And Jehoshaphat bowed his head with his face to the

ground: and all Judah and the inhabitants of Jerusalem fell before the LORD, worshipping the LORD.

19 And the Levites, of the children of the Kohathites, and of the children of the Korhites, stood up to praise the LORD God of Israel with a loud voice on high.

20 And they rose early in the morning, and went forth into the wilderness of Tekoa: and as they went forth, Jehoshaphat stood and said, Hear me, O Judah, and ye inhabitants of Jerusalem; Believe in the LORD your God, so shall ye be established; believe his prophets, so shall ye prosper.

21 And when he had consulted with the people, he appointed singers unto the LORD, and that should praise the beauty of holiness, as they went out before the army, and to say, Praise the LORD; for his mercy endureth for ever.

What happens when you praise God in the middle of your trial? What could possibly happen if you dare to glorify Him when your suffering is greatest? At the time when most people would be afraid, if you lift your voice and begin to bless the Lord, instead blaming Him for your situation, what do you think God will do about your problem? Let's see what He did for them:

22 And when they began to sing and to praise, the LORD set ambushments against the children of Ammon, Moab, and mount Seir, which were come against Judah; and they were smitten.

23 For the children of Ammon and Moab stood up against the inhabitants of mount Seir, utterly to slay and destroy them: and when they had made an end of the inhabitants of Seir, every one helped to destroy another.

24 And when Judah came toward the watch tower in the wilderness, they looked unto the multitude, and, behold, they were dead bodies fallen to the earth, and none escaped.

25 And when Jehoshaphat and his people came to take away the spoil of them, they found among them in abundance both riches with the dead bodies, and precious jewels, which they

27

stripped off for themselves, more than they could carry away: and they were three days in gathering of the spoil, it was so much.

26 And on the fourth day they assembled themselves in the valley of Berachah; for there they blessed the LORD: therefore the name of the same place was called, The valley of Berachah, unto this day.

27 Then they returned, every man of Judah and Jerusalem, and Jehoshaphat in the forefront of them, to go again to Jerusalem with joy; for the LORD had made them to rejoice over their enemies.

28 And they came to Jerusalem with psalteries and harps and trumpets unto the house of the LORD.

29 And the fear of God was on all the kingdoms of those countries, when they had heard that the LORD fought against the enemies of Israel.

30 So the realm of Jehoshaphat was quiet: for his God gave him rest round about.

31 And Jehoshaphat reigned over Judah: he was thirty and five years old when he began to reign, and he reigned twenty and five years in Jerusalem. And his mother's name was Azubah the daughter of Shilhi.

32 And he walked in the way of Asa his father, and departed not from it, doing that which was right in the sight of the LORD.

God did not fail Jehoshaphat, and He won't fail you. Just like the people of Judah, let us lift up the name of the Lord, let us give praise to God and thank him for boosting our God-esteem. I want you to think about a problem or a situation that you are going through right now. If you are not going through anything, then think of a problem or prayer request you know someone else has, and let's cast all our cares on the Lord. Believe in your heart that God is greater than the problem or the situation. Rise above the pain and know that He will work things out all right. Let's praise Him in advance for what He is going to do. Most of all, praise Him just for who He

28

is, and how much we esteem him in our hearts. He is a great, wonderful God, worthy of all the praise and all the glory, and **HE WON'T FAIL!**

Take a moment right now and pray this prayer:
Lord, forgive me for the negative ideas and attitudes that I have received about you from the enemy. Heal my hurts, heal my pain. I know that trials and situations come to make me strong. I may not understand everything, but Lord I know you do love me. Work on my attitude. Increase my God-esteem. Help my attitude to reflect faith that you are in control, and you are working things out for my good. In Jesus' matchless name, Amen!

Enthusiasm is the fire of high God-esteem

When you lay hold to the promises of God and really believe what He has said, you cannot help but change your attitude for the better. The resulting enthusiasm is a passion that will infect others, and help you live a victorious life. It will help you rise above your pain and fly into the atmosphere of your destiny. Your enthusiasm and new attitude may be a put off to some. They may say, is he/she really real? Well the answer is "Yes, just as real as God is, and I know I have his unmerited favor, no matter what the situation!"

Let me share with you some quotes on enthusiasm:

"Enthusiasm is faith set on fire"
~ George Adams

"Nothing great was ever achieved without enthusiasm."
~ Ralph Waldo Emerson

"How do you go from where you are to where you want to be? I think you have to have an enthusiasm for life. You have to have a dream, a goal. You have to be willing to work for it."

29

~ Jim Valvano

"No one keeps his enthusiasm automatically. Enthusiasm must be nourished with new actions, new aspirations, new efforts, new vision." ~ Papyrus

"The worst bankruptcy in the world is the person who has lost his enthusiasm" ~ H. W. Arnold

Enthusiasm Defined:

Main Entry: **en·thu·si·asm**
Pronunciation: in-'thü-zE-"a-z&m, en-, *also* -'thyü-
Function: noun
Etymology: Greek enthousiasmos, from enthousiazein to be inspired, irregular from entheos inspired, from en- + theos god
1 : belief in special revelations of the Holy Spirit
2 a : strong excitement of feeling : **ARDOR b :** something inspiring zeal or fervor
synonym see PASSION[6]

    The roots of this word essentially mean divine inspiration. To be inspired by God is to develop the mind of God, the attitude of God, and to be fueled with the passion of His ideas. As your God-esteem increases, your thinking will be blessed, so your actions will be blessed, and your life will be blessed - all by giving your attitude over to the Lord and allowing Him to renew your mind. It is impossible to be enthusiastic and depressed simultaneously. You must choose one or the other. CHOOSE your attitude! This is key to rising above the pain of your problems. CHOOSE!!!

*   *   *

---

[6] Source: http://www.m-w.com/cgi-bin/dictionary

A Biblical Woman Who Rose Above The Pain:

-THE SYROPHENICIAN WOMAN-

Where To Find Her In The Word:
Matthew 15:21-28

Who She Was:

Matthew 15:21, 22

[21] Then Jesus went thence, and departed into the coasts of Tyre and Sidon.
[22] And, behold, a woman of Canaan came out of the same coasts, and cried unto him, saying, Have mercy on me, O Lord, thou son of David; my daughter is grievously vexed with a devil.

Here is a mother in pain. Many women would rather have trouble fall on them if it meant that their children would be spared. A mother's love is a sacrificial one, and true mothers will do anything to help their children. Notice here, she said 'have mercy on me.....thou son of David'. She knew his lineage. Her faith told her he was the messiah. She believed that he could help her.

Her Pain:

Matthew 15:23-26

[23] But he answered her not a word. And his disciples came and besought him, saying, Send her away; for she crieth after us.
[24] But he answered and said, I am not sent but unto the lost sheep of the house of Israel.
[25] Then came she and worshipped him, saying, Lord, help me.

31

26But he answered and said, It is not meet to take the children's bread, and to cast it to dogs

Can you imagine? He ignored her! Then He told her He was not here to help her! Sometimes God says no. Sometimes God says wait. Do you have enough God-esteem to keep you when God says something you don't want to hear? She did! What did she do? She **worshipped** him! She kept asking for help. Read on to see how she answered Him when He said it was not fitting for Him to help her:

How She Rose Above It:

Matthew 15:27, 28

27And she said, Truth, Lord: yet the dogs eat of the crumbs which fall from their masters' table.
28Then Jesus answered and said unto her, O woman, great is thy faith: be it unto thee even as thou wilt. And her daughter was made whole from that very hour.

She did not argue with God. By most people's sensibilities, the Lord had said a harsh thing to her. We don't always understand why God says or does what He does. But God is sovereign. He is omnipotent and omnipresent. He knows the end from the beginning. He knew this woman's heart. He knew her faith, and he knew she could take what he said to her. Are you in a trial, or tribulation? God knows you better than you know yourself. He has counted you worthy to go through it. He is molding you and making you, and He is showing those around you the strength of your character. This woman showed what she was made of. She first agreed with her Savior, and then she pointed out another truth, and her faith touched His heart. God is truth, and He cannot deny Himself. God responds to faith. Faith is what pleases Him; faith

32

in spite of the circumstances, and faith that withstands the storms of life. Her faith made her daughter whole, and your faith will fix it for you too!

*   *   *

SUFFERING FROM PEOPLE

Many times in our lives, people are a source of pain and suffering. Songs have been written about it, usually containing words like: "I've been talked about, I've been criticized, I have wiped many tears from my eyes....". If you live long enough, someone somewhere is going to say or do something to hurt your feelings, or make you feel small, or otherwise cause you to suffer. If you have the unfortunate happenstance of being a person that cares too much about what people think, then that suffering will be intensified.

The enemy of your soul enjoys using people to offset you. Often, the very people who you would think would be with you can do things to hurt you. How do you deal with this? How do you handle it in a way that pleases God, and helps you cope?

First, you must realize who the real enemy is. It is not the flesh and blood human being causing the problem. It is Satan, the enemy of both of your souls, that is at work.

Ephesians 6:11-13
[11]Put on the whole armour of God, that ye may be able to stand against the wiles of the devil.

[12]For we wrestle not against flesh and blood, but against principalities, against powers, against the rulers of the darkness of this world, against spiritual wickedness in high places.

[13]Wherefore take unto you the whole armour of God, that ye may be able to withstand in the evil day, and having done all, to stand.

34

You must keep on the whole armor of God in order to withstand the enemy's attack. Truth, righteousness, the gospel of peace, faith, salvation, the Spirit, The Word, and watching and praying, are all important weapons for the saved soldier's arsenal. (see Ephesians chapter 6). If you know truth is on your side, if you are walking righteously, if you follow peace with all men, if you have faith, if you are truly saved, if you abide in the word of God, and continue watching and praying, you will be able to stand against the attack of the enemy. You will also be able to forgive the person who wronged you, remembering that temperance and longsuffering are fruit of the Spirit.

I Peter 2:19-24

[19] For this is thankworthy, if a man for conscience toward God endure grief, suffering wrongfully.

[20] For what glory is it, if, when ye be buffeted for your faults, ye shall take it patiently? but if, when ye do well, and suffer for it, ye take it patiently, this is acceptable with God.

[21] For even hereunto were ye called: because Christ also suffered for us, leaving us an example, that ye should follow his steps:

[22] Who did no sin, neither was guile found in his mouth:

[23] Who, when he was reviled, reviled not again; when he suffered, he threatened not; but committed himself to him that judgeth righteously:

[24] Who his own self bare our sins in his own body on the tree, that we, being dead to sins, should live unto righteousness: by whose stripes ye were healed.

Follow in the steps of Christ! When people inflict suffering, do not be overcome of evil, but overcome evil with good! Understand that you are blessed when you are tested in this way. If no one is talking about you, and you never go through with people, perhaps you are doing something wrong. If you are truly following Christ and doing spiritual exploits for the kingdom of God, then somewhere, somehow, someone is going to criticize. Just make sure they are incorrect in their assumptions or statements about you. Make sure their self-righteous ranting and ravings are not valid. Check yourself. If you know that you are blameless, then count it all joy when you are criticized for righteousness sake! Our Lord Jesus Christ was one of the most misunderstood people on the face of the earth - right up until they crucified Him. Even today He is still misunderstood. Why do we then think that we should be exempt from this kind of adversity? If we live like Jesus we can count on it happening to us as well.

The fact of life is that human beings are flawed. This is why we need salvation. People have hang ups, problems, preconceived notions. Narrow-mindedness is common. You cannot live life for people. You must live it for God. Jesus knew His calling; He knew what He had to do to save our souls. All of the suffering He endured at Calvary was inflicted by people. **All of it!**

Matthew 5:11-12

[11]Blessed are ye, when men shall revile you, and persecute you, and shall say all manner of evil against you falsely, for my sake.

[12]Rejoice, and be exceeding glad: for great is your reward in heaven: for so persecuted they the prophets which were before you

1 Peter 3:14-17

¹⁴But and if ye suffer for righteousness' sake, happy are ye: and be not afraid of their terror, neither be troubled; ¹⁵But sanctify the Lord God in your hearts: and be ready always to give an answer to every man that asketh you a reason of the hope that is in you with meekness and fear: ¹⁶Having a good conscience; that, whereas they speak evil of you, as of evildoers, they may be ashamed that falsely accuse your good conversation in Christ. ¹⁷For it is better, if the will of God be so, that ye suffer for well doing, than for evil doing.

As the Word tells us, it is better to suffer for doing the right thing than for doing the wrong thing. But what if you *have* done wrong?

If you are to gain total victory, and rise above your pain, we must address this issue as well. What if you have brought suffering upon yourself because of your actions? What if people persecute you because you **have** made some mistakes? What if those who enjoy pointing fingers at you are doing so because of what you **have** done? How do you conquer the bondage they have tried to put you in? How do you overcome the guilt and shame? How do you overcome the suffering they have inflicted and rise above the pain?

1. **Repent.** Get down on your knees and ask the Lord to forgive you for your wrongdoing. Turn away from your sin. Make a change. You cannot change others, but you can change yourself. Begin to do right, and keep doing right no matter what.

2. **Apologize to those you have wronged.** If you have wronged someone, the best thing to do is to admit you have done wrong and ask for their forgiveness. Don't let pride get in the way. We are talking about your soul. Hell is not worth your pride. If you are wrong, apologize.

37

3. **Understand that the enemy of your soul is just using your critics to try to keep you ashamed.** ALL HAVE SINNED. ALL HAVE COME SHORT. The Word tells us no one is good in his/her own right. We are all saved by grace. If the prince of this world can keep you prisoner in your mind about your mistakes, he will keep you from healing and stepping boldly forth to help others overcome by the word of your testimony. Also, remember that once you have repented your critics are committing sin by being self righteous and unmerciful. They probably need your prayers more than they know. Pray that they will be delivered from this detrimental sin. Praying for them will also help you to forgive them, and help prevent you from being angry or bitter against them.

4. **Refuse to let what others have to say define who you are.** You are not a prisoner of your past! Jesus Christ paid the price for your sin at Calvary and his blood has set you free. You have ONE master, the Lord Jesus Christ, and it is in His eyes that you stand or you fall. If you have been to the throne of grace and have apologized to those you have wronged, then stand strong in the Lord!

Ephesians 6:10

[10]Finally, my brethren, be strong in the Lord, and in the power of his might.

Isaiah 54:17

[17]No weapon that is formed against thee shall prosper; and every tongue that shall rise against thee in judgment thou shalt condemn. This is the heritage of the servants of the LORD, and their righteousness is of me, saith the LORD.

Once God has forgiven you, and you have forgiven yourself - **MOVE ON!** Your heritage is to be the head and not the tail. Your critics are irrelevant. They cannot prosper in their persecution of you as long as you walk upright. Treat them with love no matter what they say or do. Turn the situation over to Jesus and keep walking in victory!

*   *   *

A Biblical Woman Who Rose Above The Pain:

- HANNAH -

Where To Find Her In The Word:
I Samuel Chapters 1 and 2

Who She Was:

I Samuel 1:1-2

¹ Now there was a certain man of Ramathaimzophim, of mount Ephraim, and his name was Elkanah, the son of Jeroham, the son of Elihu, the son of Tohu, the son of Zuph, an Ephrathite:
² And he had two wives; the name of the one was Hannah, and the name of the other Peninnah: and Peninnah had children, but Hannah had no children.

Hannah was one of two wives of a man named Elkanah. Peninnah, Elkanah's first wife, had children, Hannah did not. The Word says that, though Hannah did not have children, Elkanah loved her, and preferred her above Peninnah, giving her a better portion every year when it was time to travel to Shiloh to worship. The jealous Peninnah taunted Hannah because she did not have children, and this caused her much pain. Hannah cried out to God year after year to give her a child. She told the Lord if He blessed her, she would give the child back to Him, to serve Him. One day, she was praying in the temple, and Eli the priest rebuked her thinking she was drunk, because she prayed moving her lips, but not speaking aloud. She told him she was not drunk, but that she was very sorrowful, and that she had poured out her heart to the Lord.

Her Pain

I Samuel 1:6-11

6   And her adversary also provoked her sore, for to make her fret, because the LORD had shut up her womb.
7   And as he did so year by year, when she went up to the house of the LORD, so she provoked her; therefore she wept, and did not eat.
8   Then said Elkanah her husband to her, Hannah, why weepest thou? and why eatest thou not? and why is thy heart grieved? am not I better to thee than ten sons?
9   So Hannah rose up after they had eaten in Shiloh, and after they had drunk. Now Eli the priest sat upon a seat by a post of the temple of the LORD.
10   And she was in bitterness of soul, and prayed unto the LORD, and wept sore.
11   And she vowed a vow, and said, O LORD of hosts, if thou wilt indeed look on the affliction of thine handmaid, and remember me, and not forget thine handmaid, but wilt give unto thine handmaid a man child, then I will give him unto the LORD all the days of his life, and there shall no razor come upon his head.

While Hannah suffered, her adversary took pleasure in taunting her, and reminding her of her circumstance. Oh what pain can be caused by a jealous heart! Hannah's pain was the endurance of that suffering.

How She Rose Above It

I Samuel 1:17-19

17   Then Eli answered and said, Go in peace: and the God of Israel grant thee thy petition that thou hast asked of him.
18   And she said, Let thine handmaid find grace in thy sight. So the woman went her way, and did eat, and her

countenance was no more sad.
19   And they rose up in the morning early, and worshipped
before the LORD, and returned, and came to their house to
Ramah: and Elkanah knew Hannah his wife; and the LORD
remembered her.

When Eli heard Hannah's story, he told her to go in peace. He agreed with her that the Lord would grant her petition. As time went by, she found herself with child, and that child was named Samuel. When Samuel was weaned, Hannah took him to Eli the prophet, and he stayed with Eli and learned the ways of the Lord; and Samuel served God. Hannah's son, Samuel, feared God, and walked in His way. He became a prophet, and upon the death of Eli, he led Israel, admonishing them to keep God's commandments. God used him to anoint Saul, Israel's first king, and subsequently, King David. What a wonderful son to have, who went on to lead a nation, and to be mightily used by God!

Instead of turning away from God because of her pain, Hannah turned toward Him, knowing that He was able to help her. Once Eli the prophet agreed with her that God would give her a child, she rose above her pain, and held on to the promise until it was fulfilled. The Word tells us that she stopped crying, went home, and ate bread. She showed high God-esteem because she was comforted by the promise of a God who's Word she knew was trustworthy. She also kept her word to God. She gave Samuel back to God when he was weaned just as she said she would. What a great sacrifice for her to finally have a child, take care of him for a while, then have to take him to live with Eli. God rewarded her for keeping her promise by giving her more children. What a mighty God we serve! Hannah definitely agrees. Here is her praise to God for answering her prayer:

1 Samuel 2:1, 2

1   And Hannah prayed, and said, My heart rejoiceth in the LORD, mine horn is exalted in the LORD: my mouth is enlarged over mine enemies; because I rejoice in thy salvation.

2   There is none holy as the LORD: for there is none beside thee: neither is there any rock like our God.

*   *   *

SUFFERING THAT COMES FROM PROBLEMS

Some days everything that can go wrong **will** go wrong. And sometimes you have no idea how you are going to solve a problem or situation. The circumstance may be totally beyond your control, and you may even be in shock and in disbelief about it. Some trials seem too difficult to bear, and some circumstances come that may leave you feeling devastated, and hopeless. This is a fact of life. I am told that an Apostle in the Church Of Our Lord Jesus Christ of the Apostolic Faith once said something like: The facts are one thing, the truth is another. The *fact* is that you are afflicted, but the *truth* is that God is going to deliver!

I Peter 4:12, 13, 16-19

[12]Beloved, think it not strange concerning the fiery trial which is to try you, as though some strange thing happened unto you:
[13]But rejoice, inasmuch as ye are partakers of Christ's sufferings; that, when his glory shall be revealed, ye may be glad also with exceeding joy.
[16]Yet if any man suffer as a Christian, let him not be ashamed; but let him glorify God on this behalf.

[17]For the time is come that judgment must begin at the house of God: and if it first begin at us, what shall the end be of them that obey not the gospel of God?

[18]And if the righteous scarcely be saved, where shall the ungodly and the sinner appear?

[19]Wherefore let them that suffer according to the will of God commit the keeping of their souls to him in well doing, as unto a faithful Creator.

He is a faithful Creator. You may not understand it right now, but you are going through for a reason. <u>God has not forgotten about you</u>, and the suffering you may be doing right now is molding you and making you more like Jesus every day. This suffering did not come to stay, it came to PASS.

Problems create suffering. Remember, suffering brings us closer to God, and makes us more like Christ. Suffering is a faith builder. The best kind of problem is one that you have absolutely no control over. These problems make the best kind of testimony. When you have no idea how you are going to make it through, and you continue to trust in God; and then He works it out right in front of your face, it is like no other experience! Problems that are totally beyond human control will teach you the most about God, and about your adversary, the devil.

Think about it, have you ever had a day when **everything** went wrong? There are days when you are bombarded with problems. The bombardment is so intense that it really seems like overkill. This is a clue! Our adversary many times doesn't know how to bother us a little bit - oh no! - he comes in "like a flood" just like the Bible says. We see an example of this in the story of Job[7]. Learn to recognize these situations as a spiritual attack. When things go *ridiculously* wrong, then you **know** that God will come to work things out. He will "lift up a standard." Remember – this is only a test! The enemy can't do anything that God does not allow him to do! He can only go so far, and it is God who draws the line.

When you look around in the aftermath of your storm, you will see that what you went through taught you much about the Savior. You will see how it molded you, how it made you, and how it helped put you in a position to help someone else in need. You will see the fruit of your labors, and your

---

[7] See Job Chapter 1

harvest will be plentiful. I find it helpful to write down situations where I have seen how God used a trial to ultimately draw me closer to Him. (That is how this book got started.) Keeping a journal can be very therapeutic, and can remind you how God brought you out in the past, giving you the faith to believe that He can bring you out of your current difficulty.

*   *   *

A Biblical Woman Who Rose Above The Pain:

-THE SHUNAMITE WOMAN-

Where To Find Her In The Word:
II Kings 4:8-36

Who She Was:

2 Kings 4:8-10

[8]And it fell on a day, that Elisha passed to Shunem, where was a great woman; and she constrained him to eat bread. And so it was, that as oft as he passed by, he turned in thither to eat bread.
[9]And she said unto her husband, Behold now, I perceive that this is an holy man of God, which passeth by us continually.
[10]Let us make a little chamber, I pray thee, on the wall; and let us set for him there a bed, and a table, and a stool, and a candlestick: and it shall be, when he cometh to us, that he shall turn in thither.

Here was a woman with a desire to do a good deed for the man of God. She wanted to be a blessing by providing him room and board whenever he was in town. This is a great example for other saved, holy women in the church. We should strive to be a blessing to those that preach the gospel, and to everyone, whether saved or unsaved. The Word tells us that if you receive a prophet in the name of a prophet you will receive a prophet's reward[8]. There is a definite blessing in helping the man of God.

So the Shunamite woman set up the room for Elisha, and one day he came to stay with her and her husband:

---

[8] See Matthew 10:41

Her Pain:

2 Kings 4:10-20

[11]And it fell on a day, that he came thither, and he turned into the chamber, and lay there.
[12]And he said to Gehazi his servant, Call this Shunammite. And when he had called her, she stood before him.
[13]And he said unto him, Say now unto her, Behold, thou hast been careful for us with all this care; what is to be done for thee? wouldest thou be spoken for to the king, or to the captain of the host? And she answered, I dwell among mine own people.
[14]And he said, What then is to be done for her? And Gehazi answered, Verily she hath no child, and her husband is old.
[15]And he said, Call her. And when he had called her, she stood in the door.
[16]And he said, About this season, according to the time of life, thou shalt embrace a son. And she said, Nay, my lord, thou man of God, do not lie unto thine handmaid.
[17]And the woman conceived, and bare a son at that season that Elisha had said unto her, according to the time of life.
[18]And when the child was grown, it fell on a day, that he went out to his father to the reapers.
[19]And he said unto his father, My head, my head. And he said to a lad, Carry him to his mother.
[20]And when he had taken him, and brought him to his mother, he sat on her knees till noon, and then died.

Now, here is a woman in pain. She did not ask for the blessing she received, but to get such a wonderful gift from God and then have it gone in an instant? Many people would not be able to bear this pain. They would be angry and blame God; their God-esteem would become non-existent. Such a trial might just be too much for some. (Thank God He knows how much we can bear!) How did she handle this situation? Read on:

How She Rose Above It:

2 Kings 4:22-27, 29-36

[22]*And she called unto her husband, and said, Send me, I pray thee, one of the young men, and one of the asses, that I may run to the man of God, and come again.*
[23]*And he said, Wherefore wilt thou go to him to day? it is neither new moon, nor sabbath. And she said, It shall be well.*
[24]*Then she saddled an ass, and said to her servant, Drive, and go forward; slack not thy riding for me, except I bid thee.*
[25]*So she went and came unto the man of God to mount Carmel. And it came to pass, when the man of God saw her afar off, that he said to Gehazi his servant, Behold, yonder is that Shunammite:*
[26]*Run now, I pray thee, to meet her, and say unto her, Is it well with thee? is it well with thy husband? is it well with the child? And she answered, It is well:*
[27]*And when she came to the man of God to the hill, she caught him by the feet: but Gehazi came near to thrust her away. And the man of God said, Let her alone; for her soul is vexed within her: and the LORD hath hid it from me, and hath not told me.*
[28]*Then she said, Did I desire a son of my lord? did I not say, Do not deceive me?*
[29]*Then he said to Gehazi, Gird up thy loins, and take my staff in thine hand, and go thy way: if thou meet any man, salute him not; and if any salute thee, answer him not again: and lay my staff upon the face of the child.*
[30]*And the mother of the child said, As the LORD liveth, and as thy soul liveth, I will not leave thee. And he arose, and followed her.*
[31]*And Gehazi passed on before them, and laid the staff upon the face of the child; but there was neither voice, nor hearing.*

49

Wherefore he went again to meet him, and told him, saying, The child is not awaked.

³²And when Elisha was come into the house, behold, the child was dead, and laid upon his bed.

³³He went in therefore, and shut the door upon them twain, and prayed unto the LORD.

³⁴And he went up, and lay upon the child, and put his mouth upon his mouth, and his eyes upon his eyes, and his hands upon his hands: and stretched himself upon the child; and the flesh of the child waxed warm.

³⁵Then he returned, and walked in the house to and fro; and went up, and stretched himself upon him: and the child sneezed seven times, and the child opened his eyes.

³⁶And he called Gehazi, and said, Call this Shunammite. So he called her. And when she was come in unto him, he said, Take up thy son.

This is an awesome example of rising above the pain. This woman spoke her situation into existence. When she was asked if everything was alright, she said "It is well". Let her example encourage you to speak, by faith, "It is well", even when things are going wrong. If our relationship with the Lord is right, we can confidently say, "It is well with my soul", even in the midst of tragedy.

This story shows us that God keeps his promises. What a test of faith this was for this Shunamite woman! She didn't have a nervous breakdown when her child died. She didn't accept the circumstance. She knew she had done right by the man of God. She had not asked for a blessing in return, but she got one, and something within her knew that God would not take away the blessing. She did not know how to fix the situation, but she knew the answer lay within the man of God. Today, we have the Holy Ghost on the inside, and Jesus Christ paid the price so we could have access to God. We can go directly to him when we feel powerless or when things go wrong. We may not know how to fix that situation, but the answer lies with God.

*   *   *

SUFFERING FROM SICKNESS

Let me share another personal testimony. I took a trip to Bermuda in 1994. I took the trip to get away after having lost my fiancé. The day I returned, I had a horrible looking rash all over my body. It was on my legs, arms, and face. My mother took one look at me and said we should go to the emergency room. The doctors took a look at me. One after another, at least five doctors came into the room and examined me. I knew something was wrong. They seemed to be at a loss as to what was happening to me. One doctor went to get a book of skin disorders and tried to match the funny looking rash to something in the book. Now, I can tell you, it is a nerve wracking thing to have five doctors standing around you, staring, flipping though a book and still seeming clueless. They decided to give me a short course of a medication called prednisone and sent me to a specialist.

I went to one of the most respected dermatologists in the Philadelphia area. The doctor took blood tests. She told me that my ANA was elevated. The ANA test is a test for lupus. She felt that I had a type of lupus that affects the skin. She told me that she was sure this was what I had, but that a biopsy would confirm the diagnosis.

I was stunned. This was early in my career as a medical life insurance underwriter. I knew what these tests meant. I understood what lupus was. I also knew how potentially life-threatening lupus could be. I told the doctor. "I am going to pray". She got a funny, patronizing look on her face and said, "Oh, ok… but I am pretty sure that is what you have" and gave me that little smile people give when they are just humoring you, that smile just in the corners of their mouths. However, young as I was, I knew what prayer could do.

I went home and prayed in my living room. I cried and I prayed, I prayed and I cried. I stretched out on the floor and I told the Lord "I don't want this disease!" I knew the medical symptoms…I went to work and looked them up. I had everything: the "butterfly rash" on my face, the positive ANA, I saw the test result myself – and I prayed, and I cried, and I prayed.

I had the biopsy done. They took two pieces of flesh from just under my collarbone. It was mildly painful. I went home with stitches, and I healed. I still have the scars.

The day came for me to get the results. I went to the dermatologist's office. She sat across her desk and told me, in a rather bewildered way, that the test was negative. She said: "I guess you don't have it!" She was clearly confused. I was beaming!! My God reversed the situation!! Of course the butterfly rash disappeared, and every subsequent ANA test I have had over the years has been negative!

Why did I have to go through that situation? So I would know God as a healer! So I would **know** that prayer changes things, and that miracles **do** happen in this day and age. Prayer is the key, and faith unlocks the door! This suffering brought me closer to my Savior. Before going through this, I could not tell someone from personal experience that God can heal you. I could tell them that the Bible says he can, but truly, there is nothing like personal experience. Now I can testify! This is how we overcome, this is how we stay strong, "by the blood of the Lamb, and the word of our testimony"[9]

You know, when I was 19 years old, I remember being in a testimony service at church. I had been saved for about four years, and I was listening to testimonies like the one I just gave about my lupus diagnosis. The testimonies seemed so sensational – hard to believe even – the horrible things people had suffered. Sickness, legal trouble, loss of loved ones, bills due, floods of problems. Each person told of a situation that seemed impossible. They told how God delivered them in incredible ways. I remember thinking to myself, "Wow, will I ever have a powerful testimony like these?" Well God must

---

[9] See Revelation 12:11

have heard that statement, and although the way may not always have been easy, I thank God for all He has taught me – even through my tests, trials, suffering, and pain. Thank you Jesus for my testimony!

*   *   *

-THE WOMAN WITH THE ISSUE OF BLOOD-

Where To Find Her In The Word:
Mark 5:25-34
Luke 8:43-48

Who She Was:

The word does not tell us her name. She is described only by the illness she endured: a twelve-year, constant issue of blood.

Her Pain:

Mark 5:25-28

²⁵ *And a certain woman, which had an issue of blood twelve years,*
²⁶ *And had suffered many things of many physicians, and had spent all that she had, and was nothing bettered, but rather grew worse,*
²⁷ *When she had heard of Jesus, came in the press behind, and touched his garment.*
²⁸ *For she said, If I may touch but his clothes, I shall be whole.*

Twelve years is a long time to be sick. Many people would have lost all hope by that time. Many would have charged God foolishly, been angry with God for making them go through that, and be bitter. But look at her God-esteem! Despite years of failure at the hands of physicians, this woman believed that Jesus could heal her! She believed it with enough fervor that she pressed to get closer to Him! We can learn from her example. We can rise above the pain when we understand that God has the answers we need, and we must get close to Him, we must reach Him and touch Him, because He will make us whole!

How She Rose Above It:

Mark 5:29-34

[29] *And straightway the fountain of her blood was dried up; and she felt in her body that she was healed of that plague.*
[30] *And Jesus, immediately knowing in himself that virtue had gone out of him, turned him about in the press, and said, Who touched my clothes?*
[31] *And his disciples said unto him, Thou seest the multitude thronging thee, and sayest thou, Who touched me?*
[32] *And he looked round about to see her that had done this thing.*
[33] *But the woman fearing and trembling, knowing what was done in her, came and fell down before him, and told him all the truth.*
[34] *And he said unto her, Daughter, thy faith hath made thee whole; go in peace, and be whole of thy plague.*

Her FAITH made her whole! That is how she rose above her pain. Through her FAITH in Jesus Christ. Nothing more needs to be said. How strong is your faith?

*   *   *

THE WILDERNESS EXPERIENCE

As saved, Christian, Holy Ghost Filled, blood washed people[10] growing in Christ, through Bible study we come to know that the Lord has promised us an inheritance (this is what the New 'Testament' is all about – our inheritance as children of God). Salvation is part of that inheritance, yes, but also many of us receive promises from the Lord in personal prayer. He may have told us that He will save our unsaved loved one; that He will bring us to a higher level of service to Him; that He will heal our body; improve our financial situation, send us a spouse, work out that personal problem we are dealing with, etc. However, we must know that His time is not our time, and there is a waiting period between the time that the promise is made and the fulfillment of that promise.

Sometimes that waiting time is difficult, especially if you do not have the correct tools/knowledge/faith to handle it. God uses that time in the "waiting room" as a test of our faith, and a tempering time. Like steel, we are tempered in the fire, but when we emerge, we are as pure gold.

Most of us know the story of the children of Israel. The Lord brought them out of the land of Egypt. They had suffered in bondage for hundreds of years. When Moses led them out of captivity it seemed their 'morning time' had come. But little did they know that the promised land was 40 years away! The Lord let them wander in the wilderness for four decades without a home or a land to call their own. They had to do this because of a lack of faith, because of murmuring and disobedience. Their suffering was prolonged because they had not learned to truly trust and obey. Having faith in God through your trial will shorten your wilderness wandering!

We can learn from the children of Israel. You may find yourself in a situation you have been in for years, and you have been waiting for a change, but it seems like the change

---

[10] See the Appendix "Are You Saved"

won't come. Have faith, believe your way though it. Trust in God. You are in the wilderness to teach you. The wilderness "waiting room" will teach you patience and determination. I like to think of a restaurant analogy: At the Waiting Room restaurant, the main dish is the fruit of longsuffering. How you digest this fruit is key to receiving its healthy benefits. Eat enough of this and you are sure to have healthy patience, and this results in healthy hope. Here is where you decide whether to quit living for God, or whether you will run on and see what the end will be. Here is where you decide if you love Him because of what He does for you, or because of who He is. I asked you this question before: Why do you serve Him? Will you stay with Him? Do you trust Him? Can He trust *you*?

The 'waiting room' experience reminds me of one of my favorite scriptures. This scripture helped get me through my wilderness:

Hebrews 10:35-39
[35] *"Cast not away therefore your confidence, which hath great recompence of reward.*

[36] *For ye have need of patience, that, after ye have done the will of God, ye might receive the promise.*

[37] *For yet a little while, and he that shall come will come, and will not tarry.*

[38] *Now the just shall live by faith: but if any man draw back, my soul shall have no pleasure in him.*

[39] *But we are not of them who draw back unto perdition; but of them that believe to the saving of the soul."*

Hold on to the promises of God! Look to the hills from whence cometh your help![11] Remember His great love for you,

---
[11] See Psalm 121

and know that whatever happens, He is right there where you are. The Holy Ghost will comfort you, and guide you. When no one else knows what to say, God knows what to say. Seek Him in prayer today and receive a blessing from Him. The key is prayer **and** praise. **With thanksgiving** make your request known to God. He **will** provide. Cast not away your confidence. Hope in God! For we know....

Romans 8:28

[28] *".......that all things work together for good to them that love God, to them who are the called according to his purpose."*

Trust the Lord, he will bring you out of the wilderness, out of the suffering, into a land flowing with milk and honey. And you will find yourself equipped with all the tools you need to go forth, possess the land, and receive the inheritance.

Deuteronomy 8:1-9

[1]*All the commandments which I command thee this day shall ye observe to do, that ye may live, and multiply, and go in and possess the land which the LORD sware unto your fathers.*

[2]*And thou shalt remember all the way which the LORD thy God led thee these forty years in the wilderness, to humble thee, and to prove thee, to know what was in thine heart, whether thou wouldest keep his commandments, or no.*

[3]*And he humbled thee, and suffered thee to hunger, and fed thee with manna, which thou knewest not, neither did thy fathers know; that he might make thee know that man doth not live by bread only, but by every word that proceedeth out of the mouth of the LORD doth man live.*

[4]*Thy raiment waxed not old upon thee, neither did thy foot swell, these forty years.*

⁵Thou shalt also consider in thine heart, that, as a man chasteneth his son, so the LORD thy God chasteneth thee.

⁶Therefore thou shalt keep the commandments of the LORD thy God, to walk in his ways, and to fear him.

⁷For the LORD thy God bringeth thee into a good land, a land of brooks of water, of fountains and depths that spring out of valleys and hills;

⁸A land of wheat, and barley, and vines, and fig trees, and pomegranates; a land of oil olive, and honey;

⁹A land wherein thou shalt eat bread without scarceness, thou shalt not lack any thing in it; a land whose stones are iron, and out of whose hills thou mayest dig brass.

Remember, when you are going through trials and tribulations, that the "trying of your faith worketh patience, and in patience you possess your souls"[12]. Trials are God's way of tempering us. Like gold, we must be tried in the fire. But once we have suffered awhile, The Word says the Lord will "make you perfect, stablish, strengthen, settle you"[13]. Once the Lord has proved us, he will bless us. He needs to know the depth of our commitment to Him, and He does know, but **we need to know too**! We need to know within ourselves that no matter what happens, our hearts are set, our minds are made up, and we are going through. We also need to know how mighty our God is to save, to heal, and to deliver. If we never went through anything, we would never know He is able to bring us out, and into our promised land. So hold on dear soldiers, hold on. When God is through with you, you will come forth, as pure gold!

*   *   *

---

[12] See James 1:3 and Luke 21:19
[13] See 1 Peter 5:10

A Biblical Woman Who Rose Above The Pain:

-THE WIDOW WOMAN-

Where To Find Her In The Word:
I Kings 17

Who She Was:

God has a heart for widows. In this scripture below we see a woman who had resigned herself to her fate. She was running out of food for herself and her son, but God stepped in:

I Kings 17:10-16

[10]*So he arose and went to Zarephath. And when he came to the gate of the city, behold, the widow woman was there gathering of sticks: and he called to her, and said, Fetch me, I pray thee, a little water in a vessel, that I may drink.*
[11]*And as she was going to fetch it, he called to her, and said, Bring me, I pray thee, a morsel of bread in thine hand.*
[12]*And she said, As the LORD thy God liveth, I have not a cake, but an handful of meal in a barrel, and a little oil in a cruse: and, behold, I am gathering two sticks, that I may go in and dress it for me and my son, that we may eat it, and die.*
[13]*And Elijah said unto her, Fear not; go and do as thou hast said: but make me thereof a little cake first, and bring it unto me, and after make for thee and for thy son.*
[14]*For thus saith the LORD God of Israel, The barrel of meal shall not waste, neither shall the cruse of oil fail, until the day that the LORD sendeth rain upon the earth.*
[15]*And she went and did according to the saying of Elijah: and she, and he, and her house, did eat many days.*

¹⁶And the barrel of meal wasted not, neither did the cruse of oil fail, according to the word of the LORD, which he spake by Elijah.

This was definitely a miracle in this woman's life. Because she put God first by feeding the prophet first, He sustained her and her son. We should always give God our best, the first fruits of our labor. If we do this, He will provide for our needs. Does this remind you of another group of people God fed and sustained? Yes – the children of Israel. He fed them with manna in the wilderness.

Now after having received this miracle in her life, this woman's God-esteem should be at an all time high. She should know, no matter what the situation, God can work things out. Let's see if her God-esteem withstood her next difficulty:

Her Pain:

I Kings 17:17, 18

¹⁷And it came to pass after these things, that the son of the woman, the mistress of the house, fell sick; and his sickness was so sore, that there was no breath left in him.
¹⁸And she said unto Elijah, What have I to do with thee, O thou man of God? art thou come unto me to call my sin to remembrance, and to slay my son?

Doesn't this sound like complaining? Murmuring? Who else murmured and complained? You know by now: The children of Israel. Just as they did, how quickly the widow seemed to forget the miracle of God in her life! However, it is clear she is speaking in reaction to two things: guilt and pain. The Bible doesn't tell us what her sins were, but clearly she thought that her son's illness and death was some kind of punishment. If you have suffered the loss of a loved one, or suffered tragedy in your life, how many times has the enemy of your soul tried to tell you that this trial is payback for your sins? This is not a new tactic of the devil, but you must recognize it and rebuke it. Jesus paid the price for your sins on Calvary. Your trials are not to punish you, but to mold you and make you into the believer that can bear much fruit for the kingdom.

How She Rose Above It:

I Kings 17:19-24

[19] And he said unto her, Give me thy son. And he took him out of her bosom, and carried him up into a loft, where he abode, and laid him upon his own bed.
[20] And he cried unto the LORD, and said, O LORD my God, hast thou also brought evil upon the widow with whom I sojourn, by slaying her son?
[21] And he stretched himself upon the child three times, and cried unto the LORD, and said, O LORD my God, I pray thee, let this child's soul come into him again.
[22] And the LORD heard the voice of Elijah; and the soul of the child came into him again, and he revived.
[23] And Elijah took the child, and brought him down out of the chamber into the house, and delivered him unto his mother: and Elijah said, See, thy son liveth.
[24] And the woman said to Elijah, Now by this I know that thou art a man of God, and that the word of the LORD in thy mouth is truth.

This woman allowed doubt and fear to come in, but God, who is rich in mercy, proved Himself and His prophet to her. How many times does God bless us, sustain us, and keep us; but then, when trouble comes, we still allow fear and doubt to come in? Yet God is full of love and mercy. Let us take a lesson from this woman. Let us acknowledge how God has blessed us in the past, and allow that faith to take us through the next trial. Let us decide now that we will trust and believe God, and know that, no matter what, if he brought us **to** it, he will bring us **through** it! I challenge you to hold onto faith and watch how quickly your wilderness will change in to a promised land!

*   *   *

RISING ABOVE THE PAIN

The inspiration for this book came in part from a workshop that I was asked to teach a few years ago. The topic was simply "Rising Above The Pain". The dear sister who asked me to speak on this topic knew that I had the testimony of overcoming the loss of my fiancé. I was still single when she asked me to come and teach the workshop. It had been about 9 years since I experienced that loss. That trial, and others I had endured since then, had made me strong.

I remember being excited about sharing what the Lord had given me for the workshop with the women. I felt I really had something to impart, and I was looking forward to my time to teach. We arrived at the conference center, checked in, and had begun attending the sessions. We were having a great time! There is something very special and wonderful about spiritual women's retreats. The bonding and sharing that occurs really builds your faith and resolve to stay with the Lord.

I remember walking to the restaurant where we were to meet to eat. In order to get there, I had to go down a few steps, through the conference center bakery, and then up steps to the restaurant. There had been a rug on the floor at the bottom of the first few steps just before getting to the bakery. I did not notice that this time, the rug was gone, and there was water on the floor. I slipped and fell and twisted my ankle. It was VERY painful! I wasn't sure if the ankle was broken or not.

I was taken by ambulance to the hospital. One of the sisters accompanied me to the hospital, and stayed with me. My ankle was x-rayed and it was determined that no bones were broken. They then bandaged the ankle, and I was sent back to the conference with crutches.

I was so anxious to get back to the conference. I was worried that I would miss giving my workshop. I felt that the whole thing was nothing but the devil trying to block me from sharing how the Lord had delivered me from trials and tribulations. I was determined that my testimony would not be stopped. When we got back to the conference I discovered that the coordinator had graciously re-arranged the scheduling so that I could still teach the workshop!

That evening, I was wheeled into the room (The conference center had given me a wheelchair), and I noticed that they had brought in a table and placed it beside the podium so I could sit and teach. The women were in full praise and worship. We sang the songs of Zion, and the anointing of the Holy Ghost filled the room. As the praises went up, I could feel the blessings coming down. When they read my biographical sketch and introduced me, I knew what I had to do.

They got me all situated to begin to teach, and in my opening remarks I thanked them for inviting me. I then made reference to my unfortunate fall, and hospital visit. I let them know that I was determined that nothing would stop this workshop. I told them that there was no way that I could sit here and talk to them about rising above the pain if I could not show them what that means. I got up, and hopped over to the podium. I left the chair and the crutches. I explained to them that I had to rise above the pain and give God the glory, and teach this workshop from the podium!

The power of my experience was evident. As the anointing moved all over the room, I began to understand that it was not the devil that caused me to sprain my ankle, it was an all wise God that had a point to make to the women in that workshop. He wanted them to understand that it is He who gives them to power to rise above the pain, and that He is the one who is going through their trials with them. Nothing can happen that He does not allow, and the adversity in our lives is just part of His plan to make us more effective vessels for Him!

I want you to understand that if you serve the most High God, then no matter what you are going through, God is right there with you. He is abiding on the inside of you. He feels what you feel. He knows what you are experiencing, and He is not taking you through anything that He is not willing to go through WITH YOU!! He will be with you in the midst of trouble, and if you keep your mind on Him, He will give you peace in spite of what is going on. I am a witness of these things. I am not writing what I think. This is what I **know** to be true! I know Him as a Heavy Load Sharer, a Healer, a Lawyer, a Friend, a Father, a Provider, and more!

ACCENTUATE THE POSITIVE

Philippians 4:7-9
[7]And the peace of God, which passeth all understanding, shall keep your hearts and minds through Christ Jesus.

[8]Finally, brethren, whatsoever things are true, whatsoever things are honest, whatsoever things are just, whatsoever things are pure, whatsoever things are lovely, whatsoever things are of good report; if there be any virtue, and if there be any praise, think on these things.

[9]Those things, which ye have both learned, and received, and heard, and seen in me, do: and the God of peace shall be with you.

There is an old song, a show tune, I heard it when I was very young, and although it is not a spiritual song, the words of the song are supported by the above scripture, and the words are a motto that has served me well. The words are: "Accentuate the positive, eliminate the negative, accentuate the positive and don't mess with Mr. In-Between"[14]. Now the

---

[14] Ac-cent-tu-ate The Positive (Mister In-Between) by Johnny Mercer and Harold Arlen

Bible says "The just shall live by faith"[15], but many times in our lives the enemy of our souls attempts to get us to take our eyes off God, and to begin looking around and walking by sight. While we are walking by sight the enemy makes sure that the sights we see will be negative and discouraging. He will be sure to show us what isn't working right, or going our way. But we have no business even looking around! We have no business trying to figure out how and when something is going to be fixed, get right, or change! Our eyes should be steadily on the Lord, our minds should be stayed on Him. Our thoughts should be thinking on all the true, honest, just, pure, lovely things that are of good report, full of virtue and worthy of praise! If we keep our eyes on Jesus, nothing will disturb our peace!

Isaiah 26:2-4
[2]Open ye the gates, that the righteous nation which keepeth the truth may enter in.

[3]Thou wilt keep him in perfect peace, whose mind is stayed on thee: because he trusteth in thee.

[4]Trust ye in the LORD for ever: for in the LORD JEHOVAH is everlasting strength:

So, resolve today that you will endeavor to keep your mind stayed on Jesus Christ our Savior. In every circumstance this day, and going forward, accentuate the positive! Eliminate the negative, and don't mess with Mr. In-Between!!

---

[15] Romans 1:17

I STILL HAVE JOY

I still have joy,
I still have joy,
After all the things I've been through
I still have joy.

I still have joy,
I still have joy,
After all the things I've been through
I still have joy!

- congregational song

As we review the words to this familiar song, we remember that suffering can be difficult. The death of loved ones, financial hardship, disappointments, heartache, and pain are all hard to bear. But remember, the race is not given to the swift, or to the strong, but to the one that endures until the end[16]. Every day may not be happy in life, but when you walk with God, He gives you a joy that transcends your circumstances. Happiness is temporary. The joy of the Holy Ghost is never-ending. God's joy endures adversity. If you have the gift of the Holy Spirit, you can remain joyful no matter what you are going through. Longsuffering is a fruit of the Spirit, and the scripture shows us God's longsuffering:

2 Peter 3:9

[9] The Lord is not slack concerning his promise, as some men count slackness; but is longsuffering to us-ward, not willing that any should perish, but that all should come to repentance.

---

[16] See Ecclesiastes 9:11 and Matthew 10:22

69

Hebrews 12:2-4

2. Looking unto Jesus the author and finisher of our faith; who for the joy that was set before him endured the cross, despising the shame, and is set down at the right hand of the throne of God.
3. For consider him that endured such contradiction of sinners against himself, lest ye be wearied and faint in your minds.
4. Ye have not yet resisted unto blood, striving against sin.

Jesus did the ultimate in suffering. No matter what has happened in our lives, we have not yet resisted to the point of the shedding of our blood in this battle against sin. When we feel weary in well doing and feel like we can't take it anymore, we should remember God's suffering; how He allowed men to shed His blood, and know that the chastisement of our peace is upon him, and with His help, and by His grace, we can take it - and if we can take it, we can make it!

**Must Jesus bear the cross alone,
and all the world go free?
No, there's a cross for everyone,
and there's a cross for me!**

-Thomas Shepherd (1693)

Yes there is a cross we all must bear. And you know what? **It is worth it all.** To know Jesus - to really KNOW Him! To draw nigh to the Lord and to have Him draw nigh to you - there is nothing more precious! I have had some fiery trials in my life, but I think it not strange....I would not trade anything for my journey thus far. I would not trade in any bereavement, any sickness, any financial hardship, or any pain - not if it meant giving up what I have learned about the Lord.

Psalms 16:11

70

11. Thou wilt shew me the path of life: in thy presence is fulness of joy; at thy right hand there are pleasures for evermore.

So, how can we conquer the negative feelings that come with suffering? We must counteract those feelings consciously and actively. Accentuate the positive and embrace joy. Let us therefore rise above our momentary suffering. Let us wear this world lightly, so that when the Lord calls us home we can cast the garment of this life away easily, we will have nothing to hold us here, no weights, no sins, no ought against another. For tomorrow is not promised to anyone! In this life we have trials, tribulations, and many afflictions, but the Lord delivers us out of them ALL! Thanks be to God who gives us the victory! He gives us joy on this side of Jordan, and the joy of the Lord is our strength! Do you ever think about how it will be when we get over the Jordan river? When we all get to heaven – what a day of rejoicing! He will wipe all tears from our eyes. There will be no more sorrow, no more pain. Jesus Christ has overcome the world! This is our blessed hope and our sweet consolation! Keep this in mind. Remember, you can make it!

**You can make it,
You can make it,
These trials that you're going through,
God's gonna show you just what to do.
So you can make it,
I really believe it today – You can make it!
I don't care what's going wrong.
God won't let it last too long.
You're not in this test alone!! You can make – You can make it!**

- Shirley Ceasar

71

THROW OUT THE SANDBAGS

When I originally thought about the theme in this book, the analogy of a hot air balloon came to me. If you have seen a hot air balloon you know that the balloon cannot rise without hot air. A fire that burns just below the mouth of the balloon heats the air, and the people ride in a basket below the fire. Generally, before the balloon takes off, it is held to the ground by a cord wrapped around a stake, and sandbags weigh it down. As the air is heated and the sandbags are thrown out, the balloon rises. When the balloon is ready to take off, the cord is cut, or the stake is taken out of the ground, freeing the cord, and the balloon takes off.

One thing is certain, if we are going to rise above the pain, we are going to have to keep the fire of the Holy Ghost burning. The Holy Ghost is a Comforter. We have to keep the joy of the Lord, because the joy of the Lord is our strength. In that hot air balloon, if the hot air cools, the balloon sinks. If we let the joy die out, if we let discouragement, or problems, or sins cool the fire, we won't be able rise above our pain.

Many times we let the fire burn, and we get on fire for God, and we get ready to rise, but then we let pain caused by people or circumstances hold us back from being all that God wants us to be. These things are like the cord that is tied to the stake. Doubt, uncertainty, not having enough faith to see past our circumstance and trust in the Lord, are all cords that keep us tied to the ground.

I mentioned before about the sandbags that are kept on the basket of the hot air balloon. These sandbags keep the balloon from rising too high. In order to go higher, some of the sandbags have to be thrown out or cut off of the basket.

The cares of this life can weigh you down. If the devil can make you take your eyes off Jesus, then he can gain a foothold to try to throw sandbags into your balloon basket. The sandbag of doubt, the sandbag of worry, the sandbag of sin, the sandbag of jealousy, the sandbag of gossip, the sandbag of low self esteem, the sandbag of strife – these are just a few things that come to weigh you down. Recognize the trick of the enemy. Be determined to live holy. Endure hardness as a good soldier. Knowing that the reward is great, both in this life and the next. God is faithful, and will remember your labor of love. If you can take it, you can make it. If you can pray you can stay. If you can fast you can last, and if you try you can RISE!!

Jesus said, "If you love me keep my commandments."[17] If you keep his commandments, He promised He will bear you up on eagles' wings. If we obey His voice, and keep His covenant, He said we will be a peculiar treasure above all people. There is a reason you bought this book and read all of it. God is in control. There are no coincidences. If you have endured much pain, it is because there is a special anointing on your life. Your trials have not been by accident. It was the perfect will of God. Everything you have been through has brought you to this point. Stretch out on faith, trust in God, and keep the fire burning. Cut the cord, throw out the sandbags, and RISE ABOVE THE PAIN!!!!

---

[17] See John 14:15

About the Author:
Michelle Olivia Smith

Michelle Olivia Smith holds a Master of Business Administration with a concentration in Human Resource Administration, and a Bachelor of Science in Business Administration with a concentration in Operations Management. She also holds the LOMA insurance designations: Fellow, Life Management Institute (FLMI) and Associate, Customer Service (ACS). She works as a life insurance underwriter, teacher and trainer; and is a skilled project coordinator. She is a licensed Senior Missionary in the Church of Our Lord Jesus Christ of The Apostolic Faith, Inc., and she has earned many credentials, certificates and awards in industry, in academia, in singing and in the Apostolic Pentecostal Church.

Mrs. Smith has been a public speaker since she was a child, and fell in love with the Word of God at the age of six years old. For over 25 years she has been actively involved in her church and community. Mrs. Smith has a heart for women's issues, and has spoken, and facilitated workshops, for many church and women's organizations and conventions. Her workshop topics have included: Saved, Single and Walking In Victory, Overcoming Jealousy, The Humble Mind, Rising Above The Pain, Is There a GAP in your AGAPE?, Don't Look Now, Your Attitude is Showing; The Attitude Workshop Series – and many more. Her seminars and workshops focus on women's issues, sisterhood unity, spiritual growth and maturity. Her goal is to edify and teach Christian women and girls to walk in victory. Mrs. Smith is also the web-missionary and owner of an online Christian resource especially for women at www.ApostolicWoman.com.

Michelle Olivia Smith has worked in the life insurance industry as a medical underwriter for over 14 years. She has given both church-related and secular presentations on diseases such as diabetes and cancer, as well as health and wellness. Wed for over two years, Mrs. Smith and her husband Samuel Titus Smith joyfully reside in Silver Spring Maryland.

Mrs. Smith will be a highlight to your women's retreat, breakfast, luncheon, or banquet. Dynamic and encouraging, she is available also as a keynote speaker for your women's group meeting, dinner, or women's service. She can and will speak to singles, married, young or old. Mrs. Smith will be happy to present one of her seminars, or speak on the appropriate theme or topic for your event. Also, her health related seminars will give your group valuable information on any medical condition.

To schedule Mrs. Smith for a speaking/teaching engagement contact her at:

Michelle Olivia Smith
P.O. Box 5332
Fredericksburg VA 22403-5332
540-710-4205 (phone)
540-878-4751 (fax)

Email: WebMissionary@ApostolicWoman.com

Visit her on the web at: www.ApostolicWoman.com

APPENDIX

Are You Saved?

This question is the most important question of your life. Consider it carefully. **Are you truly saved?** If you should die today, or if Christ were to rapture the church today, would you go with Jesus? Do you have eternal life? Or would you wake up in Hell, or be left behind?

Do you faithfully attend a church or a synagogue, but you have a nagging feeling that just wont go away, that something is not right? Do you feel that when you 'prayed the sinners prayer' or when you went up to 'join the church', and the church voted you in, and your name was put on the roll, that you still didn't feel any different, and somewhere deep inside you knew something was missing?

Or have you never been in church, know little or nothing about the Bible, but you know that you want to know God, to really *know* Him, because you know that your life would be better off if you could just find God?

I want you to know that the Bible's plan of salvation is clear; the Word of God clearly shows what is needed to reconcile man back to God. Many people fail to truly read the Bible for themselves, to take the time to see what it is saying. They trust the preacher, the priest, or the rabbi to know all about it, and get it to them. But your soul's salvation is too important for you to leave to someone else to handle. You need to look in the Word of God and see the truth for yourself. The truth will make you free! May I suggest that you prayerfully and carefully consider the scriptures listed on the next few pages:

"Then Peter said unto them, Repent, and be baptized every one of you in the name of Jesus Christ for the remission of sins, and ye shall receive the gift of the Holy Ghost. For the promise is unto you, and to your children, and to all that are afar off, even as many as the Lord our God shall call."
- Acts 2:38, 39

You may have heard or read this scripture before. I like to call it a 'cornerstone' scripture. It sums up a critical point that affects every human being on earth. Salvation is not attained in any other way in the dispensation of grace that we are living in today. One MUST:

REPENT of your sins.

This means to turn away from, and have a godly sorrow concerning, the practice of sin.

Be BAPTIZED in the Name of Jesus Christ.

This is essential for the remission (forgiveness) of the sins you have repented (turned away) from. This baptism must be by full immersion in water, and must be in the Name of JESUS CHRIST.

"Be it known unto you all, and to all the people of Israel, that by the name of Jesus Christ of Nazareth, whom ye crucified, whom God raised from the dead, even by him doth this man stand here before you whole. Neither is there salvation in any other: for there is none other name under heaven given among men whereby we must be saved." - Acts 4:10-12

Receive the gift of the HOLY GHOST.

This is the spiritual baptism that is evidenced by the speaking in other tongues (languages) as the Spirit of God gives the utterance. The baptism of the Holy Ghost is ESSENTIAL for salvation.

"Jesus answered, Verily, verily, I say unto thee, Except a man be born of water and of the Spirit, he cannot enter into the kingdom of God." St. John 3:5

There are many instances in the Bible where people received salvation. Consider the following Biblical accounts:

The Gentiles receive the Holy Ghost:

"While Peter yet spake these words, the Holy Ghost fell on them which heard the word. And they of the circumcision which believed (the Jewish people who were saved) were astonished, as many as came with Peter, because that on the Gentiles also was poured out the gift of the Holy Ghost. For they heard them speak with tongues and magnify God. Then answered Peter, Can any man forbid water, that these should not be baptized, which have received the Holy Ghost as well as we? And he commanded them to be baptized in the name of the Lord. Then prayed they him to tarry certain days." - Acts 10:44-48

Paul's trip to Ephesus:

"And it came to pass, that, while Apollos was at Corinth, Paul having passed through the upper coasts came to Ephesus: and finding certain disciples, He said unto them, Have ye received the Holy Ghost since ye believed? And they said unto him, We have not so much as heard whether there be any Holy Ghost. And he said unto them, Unto what then were ye baptized? And they said, Unto John's baptism. Then said Paul, John verily baptized with the baptism of repentance, saying unto the people, that they should believe on him which should come after him, that is, on Christ Jesus. When they heard this, they were baptized in the name of the Lord Jesus. And when Paul

had laid his hands upon them, the Holy Ghost came on them; and they spake with tongues, and prophesied. And all the men were about twelve." - Acts 19:1-7

As you can see, those who received salvation in the Bible **repented,** were baptized **in the Name of Jesus Christ** for the remission of their sins, and **received the Holy Ghost.** This was how they became children of God.

Once they were saved, they had the power to live a holy and upright life before God. You see, you can't live holy without the Holy Ghost, and you can't get the Holy Ghost without repentance and faith toward God. You are commanded by God's holy Word, as a profession of your repentance and faith, to be baptized in water in the name of Jesus Christ.

Now that you have heard the Bible plan of salvation, make up in your mind that you will find a church that believes in the baptism in Jesus' name, and the baptism of the Holy Ghost with the evidence of speaking in other tongues. An Apostolic Pentecostal church is where we recommend you go to be taught, prayed for, and encouraged to receive the Holy Ghost. You can also receive the Holy Ghost right where you are. Begin to pray, repent of your sins, and seek God, begin to praise Him for all that He has done for you, and you may soon find yourself filled with the Holy Ghost, speaking in other tongues right where you are! You still must find a Spirit-Filled church to worship the Lord in Spirit and in truth. We can recommend churches in your area. Send your city and state via email to: WebMissionary@apostolicwoman.com . Even if you have found a church home, if this book has been instrumental in guiding you to salvation, I would love to hear from you!

God Bless You!